Illuminated Remembrance of God

Also by Imam Fode Drame

The Splendors of Quran: English Translation of the Quran
Expansions Volume 1: The Purpose of Creation
Expansions Volume 2: The Way is Peace
Expansions Volume 3: The Awakening
Expansions Volume 4: The Rejuvenation of the Soul
Expansions Volume 5: The 99 Names of Allah

Magazine
Al Qalam Magazine

Website
www.zawiyah.ca

Videos Archives
www.youtube.com/zawiyahfoundation

Live Dhikr Majlis
Listen to the Remembrance of God
www.livestream.com/zawiyahfoundation/dhikrmajlis

Live Classes, Talks, and Events
www.livestream.com/zawiyahfoundation

Illuminated
REMEMBRANCE OF GOD

Imam Fode Drame

Tasleem Publications
Vancouver, Canada

TASLEEM PUBLICATIONS
www.expansions.ca
Illuminated Remembrance of God

I. Spirituality
II. Personal Development

CONTENTS

بِسْمِ اللهِ الرَّحْمٰنِ الرَّحِيْمِ

Preface

The litanies (*adhkār*) in this collection called *Illuminated Remembrance*, were not randomly sectioned. Quite the contrary, each litany constitutes an organic part of the whole. Therefore, the sequence as well as the number of times each litany is recited must be rigorously followed. This is because not following the prescribed order will significantly interfere with the effect these litanies are supposed to produce.

This collection is intended for general and specific uses. Anyone can use it and benefit from it without any special permission as long as they respect the order of the litanies. However, obtaining a special permission (*idhn*) brings forth special benefits. We will this leave that each individual's discretion.

Additionally, it is fine to recite these litanies in solo. However, it is recommended to do them in unison with others, as the prophetic saying states, "God's hand is with the group" and "unity is mercy."

Our last invocation: All praise is for Allah the Lord of the worlds.

Imam Fode Drame

July 8, 2017

INTRODUCTION

REMEMBRANCE OF ALLAH

Dhikru-llāh or remembrance of Allah, is any practice that is intended to bring the memory of Allah back to the recollection of the rememberer, or the *dhākir*. The remembrance of Allah is therefore assumed to be about something that the *dhākir* already knew, but has forgotten. It only stands to reason that you remember what you already knew, not something you have never known.

What is it then that human beings knew, but have forgotten? The answer to this question can be gleaned from various verses in the Quran. For example, in chapter *The Cattle*, Abraham reminds his people about something they knew from the beginning but have forgotten about, namely, the all encompassing knowledge of Allah. Hence the interrogative remark of Abraham:

> [...] My Lord encompasses everything in knowledge, why then, do you not remember? (The Quran, chapter *The Cattle*, 6:80)

In this verse, Abraham reminds his people, *you did indeed know God's knowledge encompassed everything but you've forgotten it.* Similarly, God says regarding the first creation:

> You did indeed know about the first creation, why then, do you not remember? (The Quran, chapter *The Great Happening*, 56:61)

As we see in this verse, remembrance always harks back to

the first time. This is especially with regards to three matters:

1. When the first time took place.
2. When the creation witnessed the all-encompassing knowledge of God for the first time.
3. When the creation witnessed the all-encompassing mercy of God for the first time.

The overall purpose of *dhikr* is to bring you back to what is knowns as *al-ḥaqq al-awwal*, the first realization or *al-dhikr al-akbar*, the greatest certitude. This means that you must remain steadfast in the practice of *dhikr* until you fully experience the realization; and after this realization, you should be steadfast in maintaining it.

DHIKR AND SHUKR

To make this collection all-rounded, it covers both the spectrums of *dhikr* and its pair *shukr* (gratitude). God will often mention them together, which signals their complementarity. *Dhikr* is meant to take one back into pre-eternity . *Shukr*, on the other hand, takes one forward into perpetuity.

A person who practices both *dhikr* and *shukr* makes a dual progress. This involves a continuous regeneration and rejuvenation of the soul. In *dhikr*, we are going in the negative, meaning that all impressions are erased until our hearts and souls become a clean slate. As we go into *shukr*, on the other hand, the positive impressions are re-instated and then multiplied. Thus, our consciousness gets filtered and reinvigorated on a cyclical basis allowing for an exponential growth. There are many verses pointing to this four dimensional growth, such as:

> Therefore remember me and I will remember you,
> and be grateful to me and do not be ungrateful.

(The Quran, chapter *The Cow*, 2:152)

In this verse, God is exhorting us to exercise both *dhikr* and *shukr* assiduously. In another verse, God says:

> And it is He who has made the night and the day to alternate for such a one who seeks to remember Allah or seeks to offer gratitude. (The Quran, Chapter *The Criterion*, 25:62)

The meaning of this verse is that we should alternate between remembrance and gratitude in the same way that God caused the night and day to alternate. Hence, no moment in the night or day should go by without finding us in one state or the other. Elsewhere, God says:

> Allah effaces what He pleases and confirms [what he pleases] and with Him is the mother of the book. (The Quran, Chapter *The Thunder*, 13:39)

This alternation between the effacing (*maḥ'w*) and confirming (*thabūt*) is the result of *dhikr*.

With that understanding, this collection of praises and glorifications is structured along the lines of *dhikr* and *shukr*. It begins with the names of God, *Al-Ḥaqq*, which has an effacing effect. It then proceeds to *Al-Ḥayy* which confirms, and then continues to the combinations of *ḥayyu*, *qayyūm*, and *lā ilāha ill Allāh*, which comprise of both effacing and confirming. This alternation between effacing and confirming leads the heart to a state of balance (*taswiyah*), at which point a spirit is blown into the individual or a collective body of people, ushering them into the zone of witnessing wherein actions of gratitude take place.

SALAWAT

Ṣalawāt, or invocation of blessings on the Prophet,

peace be upon him, is considered as an act of gratitude. It is reported in an authentic tradition that the Prophet, peace be upon him, said: "Whoever invokes Allah's blessings (*ṣalawāt*) once upon me, Allah will send ten blessings on him." Furthermore, God instructed His Messenger Muhammad, peace be upon him, to also invoke His blessings on the believers, while pointing out one specific benefit of *ṣalawāt* on the believers, which is, tranquility (*sakīnah*):

> [...] Do invoke blessings on them, for your invocation does bring tranquility (*sakīnah*) upon them. And Allah is All Hearing All Knowing. (The Quran, Chapter *The Repentance*, 9:103).

The second benefit of *ṣalawāt* is that is produces mercy (*raḥmah*) for the invoker:

> The are the ones upon whom there will be blessings (*ṣalawāt*) and mercy (*raḥmah*) from their Lord, and they are the ones who are rightly guided. (The Quran, Chapter *The Cow*, 2:157)

THE PROPHET'S MOTHERHOOD

The Prophet, peace be upon him, hereby plays the role of motherhood (*ummiyyah*) for the believers. The three most salient characteristics of motherhood are 1. Tranquility (*sakīnah*) 2. Tenderness (*ra'fah*), fondness (*'affiyy*), affection, (*mawaddah*), and 3. Mercy (*raḥmah*). These three characteristics constitute the fundamental principals of motherhood, and the Prophet, peace be upon him, is the universal mother in whom all these principles were perfected. The following verses make this point apparent

> And We have not sent you except as mercy (*raḥmah*) to the worlds. (The Quran, Chapter *The Prophets*, 21:107)

> [...] He is keen about you, and he is full of tenderness (*ra'ūfun*) and mercy for the believers. (The Quran, Chapter *The Repentance*, 9:128)

> [...] Do invoke blessings on them, for your invocation does bring tranquility (*sakīnah*) upon them. And Allah is All Hearing All Knowing. (The Quran, Chapter *The Repentance*, 9:103)

This means that the Prophet is the source and substance of these three principles. Further, a single verse in chapter *The Romans* vividly captures this:

> And among His signs is that He created for you from yourselves mates that you may find tranquility in them and He has made between you affection and mercy. Indeed in that are signs for people who reflect. (The Quran, Chapter *The Romans*, 30:21)

The term, "from yourselves" recalls the term, "a messenger from your own selves." *From your own selves*, means part of you, a piece from you. In other words, you are a part of him and he is a part of you. He yearns for you and you yearn for him, like a part yearns for the whole and the whole for the part. Neither will find rest until they are united with the other. This union brings tranquility to both parties, and from that tranquility comes affection and mercy.

These three principles of motherhood (*ummiyyah*) are also regrouped under the generic term "*mann*," which is often translated as favour or honesty. It must therefore be borne in mind that each time God uses the word "*mann*" He is referring to the triple blessings of *sakīnah* (tranquility), *mawaddah*, *ra'fah* (affection) and *raḥmah* (mercy) as stated in the following verses:

> Allah indeed favoured (*manna*) the believers when

He sent a messenger among them from themselves. [...] (The Quran, Chapter *The Family of 'Imran*, 3:164)

[...] He is keen about you, and he is full of tenderness (*ra'ūfun*) and mercy for the believers. (The Quran, Chapter *The Repentance*, 9:128)

الصَّلَاةُ الْفَاتِحِ

OPENING PEACE AND BLESSINGS ON THE PROPHET

RECITE THREE TIMES

اللَّهُمَّ صَلِّ عَلَى سَيِّدِنَا مُحَمَّدٍ الْفَاتِحِ لِمَا أُغْلِقَ وَ

الخَاتِمِ لِمَا سَبَقَ نَاصِرِ الْحَقِ بِالْحَقِ وَالْهَادِي إِلَى

صِرَاطِكَ الْمُسْتَقِيمِ وَعلَى آلِهِ حَقَّ قَدرِهِ وَمِقْدَارِهِ

الْعَظِيمِ

Allahumma ṣalli 'alā sayyidinā muhammadin-il-fātiḥi limā ukhliqa wal khātimi limā sabaqa nāṣiri-l-ḥaqqi bi-l-ḥaqqi wa-l-hādī ilā sirāṭika-l-mustaqīm wa 'ala ālihi haqqa qadrihi wa miqdārihi-l-'ẓīm.

O Allah send your blessing on our leader Muhammad, the Opener of what was closed and the seal of what went before, the helper of truth by the Truth and the guide to Your straight path and upon his family as he deserves in truth and according to his great worth.

ذكر الله

REMEMBRANCE OF ALLAH

RECITE ACCORDING TO ALLOCATED AMOUNT

يَا حَقُّ بِالْحَقِّ حَقِّقْنِي

Yā Ḥaqqu Bil-Ḥaqqi Haqqiqni **50**
O Truth by the Truth make me true

يَا حَقُّ

Yā Ḥaqq **100**
O Truth

حَقُّ

Ḥaqq **100**
Truth

اللهُ اللهُ حَقُّ

Allāhū Allāh Ḥaqq **50**
Allah Allah is True

اللهُ حَقُّ

Allāh Ḥaqq **50**
Allah is True

اللهُ حَيٌّ

Allāh Ḥayy **50**
Allah is Ever-Living

حَيٌّ

Ḥayy **100**
Ever-Living

يَا حَيُّ يَا قَيُّوْمُ

Yā Hayyū Yā Qayyūm **50**
O Ever-Living, O All-Sustaining

سُبْحَانَ اللهِ أَسْتَغْفِرُ اللهَ

SubḥānAllāh Astaghfirullāh **50**
Glory be to Allah, I seek forgiveness from Allah

لاَ إِلَهَ إِلاَّ اللهُ

Lā ilāha illallāh **100**
There is no deity except Allah

يَا اللهُ يَا رَحْمَنُ صَلِّ عَلَى مُحَمَّدِنَا

Yā Allāh Yā Rahmān ṣalli 'alā Muḥammadinā **11**
O Allah, O All-Merciful,
Send down your blessings on our Muhammad

يَا اللهُ يَا رَحْمَنُ صَلِّ عَلَى نَبِيِّنَا

Yā Allāh Yā Raḥmān ṣalli 'alā Nabīyyinā **11**
O Allah, O All-Merciful,
Send down your blessings on our Prophet

يَا اللهُ يَا رَحْمَنُ صَلِّ عَلَى رَسُولِنَا

Yā Allāh Yā Raḥmān ṣalli 'alā Rasūlinā **11**
O Allah, O All-Merciful,
Send down your blessings on our Messenger

يَا اللهُ يَا رَحْمَنُ صَلِّ عَلَى حَبِيبِنَا

Yā Allāh Ya Raḥmān ṣalli 'alā Ḥabībinā **11**
O Allah, O All-Merciful,
Send down your blessings on our Beloved

يَا اللهُ يَا رَحْمَنُ صَلِّ عَلَى مُحَمَّدِ بَا

Yā Allāh Ya Raḥman ṣalli 'alā Muhammadibā **11**
O Allah, O All-Merciful, Send down your blessings on the soul of Muhammad.

قصيدة البردة

QASIDAH AL-BURDAH

POEM OF THE CLOAK
by Ka'ab bin Zuhair

Poetry has long been a key feature of Arab culture. It has served as a means for individuals to defend their tribes' honor, praise those they revere, as well as spread their personal views and leave a mark on society. The Arabic word *qaṣidah* describes a classical Arabic poem in which every line rhymes while maintaining a single, elaborate, meter.

During the time of the Prophet Muhammad, peace and blessings be upon him, there were at least two companions, Hassan bin Thabit and Ka'ab bin Zuhair, who excelled in reciting poetry on behalf of the young Muslim community, may God be pleased with them both. Their poems defended Islam from its enemies' hateful words and praised the beauty and virtues of the faith, God and the Prophet Muhammad, peace and blessings be upon him.

The famous name *al-Burdah* – the Cloak – comes from the first *qaṣidah* recited by Ka'ab bin Zuhair after entering Islam. Before his conversion, Ka'ab was a powerful poet for the Meccan polytheists and he had recited many poems defaming Islam and the Muslims. Ka'ab's poetry was so incendiary that the Prophet Muhammad, peace and blessings be upon him, ordered his execution if he were caught by Muslim hands.

After accepting God's oneness and the Prophet Muhammad as God's messenger, peace and blessings be upon him, Ka'ab wanted to meet the Beloved Messenger of Allah despite the mandate against his life. Following the advice of his Muslim brothers, Ka'ab decided to attend *fajr* prayer at the Prophet's mosque – *al-Masjid al-Nabawiyy* – and to disguised himself by dressing in a loose fitting, full-body cloak. After the prayer, Ka'ab came in front of the Prophet Muhammad, peace and blessings be upon him, and began to recite a *qaṣidah* praising him and seeking his forgiveness. After hearing the poem, the Prophet, peace be upon him, was delighted and so he removed his own cloak and placed it over Ka'ab's shoulders as gift. The poem's namesake – *al-burdah* – refers both to Ka'ab's disguise and the Prophet's magnanimous gesture.

Roughly seven hundred years after the Prophet Muhammad's death, peace and blessings be upon him, a second poem entitled *al-Burdah* was composed in praise of the beloved Messenger. After an illness left half of his body paralyzed, Imam Sharaf al-Din al-Busiri, may Allah have mercy on him, composed a *qaṣidah* expressing his love for the Prophet Muhammad, praising him and seeking God's mercy through his intercession. Afterwards, Imam al-Busiri saw the Prophet Muhammad, peace and blessings be upon him, in a dream – an event which, due to its magnitude, the Islamic tradition recognizes as undoubtedly true. In his vision, Imam al-Busiri recited his *qaṣidah* to the Prophet, after which the Messenger, peace and blessings be upon him, placed his cloak over him, as he had done to Ka'ab bin Zuhair centuries earlier. When Imam al-Busiri awoke, he found himself cured of his paralysis. News of his experience spread, and his *qaṣidah* became known as *Qaṣidah al-Burdah*, and is still recited frequently around the Muslim world.

The following are excerpts from the original *Qaṣidah al-Burdah* by Ka'ab bin Zuhair, may Allah be pleased with him.

قصيدة البردة

POEM OF THE CLOAK

RECITE EACH COUPLET ONCE

نُبِّئْتُ أَنَّ رَسُولَ اللهِ أَوْعَدَنِي
وَالْعَفْوُ عِنْدَ رَسُولِ اللهِ مَأْمُولْ

Nubbi'tu anna Rasūlullāhi aw'adanī
wal 'afwū 'inda rasulillāhi ma'mūl

I have been informed that the messenger has warned me
yet pardon from the messenger of Allah is expected (hoped for)

مَهْلاً هَدَاكَ الَّذِي أَعْطَاكَ نَافِلَةَ الْقُرْآنِ
فِيهَا مَوَاعِيظُ وتَفْصِيلْ

Mahlan hadāk alladhī a'ṭāka nāfilata-l Qur'āna
fihā mawā'īẓu wa tafsīl

Gently tarry you have been well-guided by the One who gave you the gift of the Quran
wherein are words of good counsel and clear guidelines

لاَ تَأْخُذَنِّي بِأَقْوَالِ الْوُشَاةِ وَلَمْ
أَذْنِبُ وَلَوْ كَثُرَتْ فِي الْأَقَاوِيلْ

La ta'khudhannī bi aqwālil wushāti wa lam
Adhnab wa law kathurat fi-l-aqāwīl

Don't hold against me the words of the detractors. I have not offended in spite of the many rumors.

لَقَدْ أَقُومُ مَقَامًا لَوْ يَقُومُ بِهِ
أَرَى وَأَسْمَعُ مَا لَوْ يَسْمَعُ الْفِيلْ

Laqad aqūmu maqāman law yaqūmu bihi
Arā wa asma'u ma law yasma'u-l-fīl

I stand in a position were to stand there,
the elephant seeing what I see and hearing what I hear

لَظَلَّ يَرْعَدُ إِلاَّ أَنْ يَكُونَ لَهُ
مِنَ الرَّسُولِ بِإِذْنِ اللهِ تَنْوِيلْ

Laẓalla yar'adu illā ay-yakūna lahu
Min ar-rasūli bi idhni-llāhi tanwīl

Would be all in tremor, unless it receives a largess from the
Messenger by God's permission

حَتَّى وَضَعْتُ يَمِينِي مَا أُنَازِعُهُ
فِي كَفِّ ذِي نَقْمَاتٍ قِيلُهُ الْقِيلْ

Hattā wada'tu yamīnī mā unāzi'uhu
Fikaffi dhī naqimātin qīluhu-l-qīl

Till I put my right hand with total resignation
in the hands of the awe-striking one whose word is final

فَلَهُوَ أَخْوَفُ عِنْدِي إِذْ أُكَلِّمُهُ
وَقِيلَ إِنَّكَ مَنْسُوبٌ وَمسْؤُولْ

Falahuwa akhwafu 'indī idh ukallimuhu
Wa qīla innaka mansūbun wa mas'ūl

He inspires me with greater awe whilst I address him, when they say that you are referred to be cross examined

مِنْ ضَيْغَمٍ بِضَرَّاءِ الْأَرْضِ مَخْدَرَهُ
فِي بَطْنِ عَثَّرَ غِيلُ دُونَهُ غِيلٌ

Min ḍayghamin bi darrā'i-l-arḍi makhdaruhu
Fi baṭni 'aththara ghīlun dūnahu ghīl

More than a lion whose den is in the thicket of the land, and in the valley of aththara a jungle behind a jungle

يَغْدُو فَيَلْحَمُ ضِرْغَامَيْنِ عَيْشُهُمَا
لَحْمٌ مِنْ النَّاسِ مَعْفُورٌ خَرَادِيل

Yaghdū fayalḥamu ḍarghāmayni 'ayshuhumā
Laḥmun min-an-nāsi ma'fūrun kharādīl

Sets out in the morning and feeds with meat, two cubs from the flesh of humans shredded and dust-ridden

إِذَا يُسَاوِرُ قِرْنًا لَا يَحِلُّ لَهُ
أَنْ يَتْرُكَ الْقِرْنَ إِلاَّ وَهُوَ مَغْلُولُ

Idhā yusāwiru qirnan lā yaḥillu lahu
an yatruka-l-qirna illā wa huwa maghlūl

If he challenges a rival it never come to pass that he would leave the opponent except in chains (fetters)

مِنْهُ تَظَلُّ سِبَاعُ الْجَوِّ نَافِرَةً
وَلَا تَمَشَّى بِوَادِيهِ الْأَرَاجِيلُ

Minhu taẓallu sibā'u-l-jawwi nāfiratan
wa lā tamashsha bi wādīhi-l-arājīl

From him the wild animals of the air fly away and men never walk about in his valley

وَلَا يَزَالُ بِوَادِيهِ أَخُو ثِقَةٍ
مُضَرَّجُ الْبَزِّ وَالدِّرْسَانُ مَأْكُولُ

Wa lā yazālu bi wādīhi akhūthiqatin
Muḍarraju-l-bazzi wa-d-dirsānu ma'kūl

How often the stout-hearted individual lay in his valley. His shirt smeared with blood his threadbare dress eaten up

إِنَّ الرَّسُولَ لَنُورٌ يُسْتَضَاءُ بِهِ
مُهَنَّدٌ مِنْ سُيُوفِ اللهِ مَسْلُولُ

Inna-r-rasūla lanūrun yustaḍā'u bihi
Muhannadun min ṣuyūfillahi maslūl

Indeed the Messenger is a light from which enlightenment is received; the unsheathed sword of God of fine Indian make.

الصَّلَاةُ الْمِنَنِيَّةُ

SALAT AL-MINANIYYAH

PRAYERS OF DIVINE BOUNTIES

The Prayers of Divine Bounties, *Ṣalat al-Minaniyyah,* is the conception and the realization of the triple principles of motherhood (*uṣūl al-ummiyyah*): *sakīnah*, *mawaddah*, and *raḥmah*. These principals also correspond to the three rights pertaining to motherhood maintained in the narration of the man who asked the messenger of Allah, peace be upon him, "Who deserves my company the most?" He said, "Your mother. Then who? Your mother. Then who? Your mother." The three rights correspond to the three blessings of motherhood (*ummiyyah*).

The *minaniyyah* captures the spirit of *ummiyyah* so that tranquility, affection, and mercy will dawn over the one who recites it. This prayer was from the Prophet, the *ummiyy* (the motherly) and it goes back to him, peace be upon him. I neither conceived or executed this *ṣalawāt*. I simply wrote down what I was inspired with.

Due to the fact that it comprises the triple principles of *ummiyyah*, the one who recites it acquits himself of his triple obligation to the Messenger of God, while acquiring triple blessings at the same time. Most often collections of invocations on the prophet focus on one of the principles, but this prayer has combined all:

> [...] He gives to whosoever he pleases, and Allah is the Master of the Most Magnificent Favor. (The Quran, chapter *The Iron*, 57:29)

الصَّلاةُ المِنَنِيَّةُ

PRAYERS OF DIVINE BOUNTIES

RECITE ENTIRE PRAYER SEVEN TIMES

اللَّهُمَّ صَلِّ عَلَى النَّبِيِّ الْأُمِّيِّ

Allahumma ṣalli alā-n-nabiyyi-l-ummiyyi

O Allah send your blessings on the Ummiyy Prophet

مَنْبَعِ الْإِمْدَادِ الْإِيمَانِي

Manba'i-l-imdādi-l-imāni

The source of (divine) provisions of faith

وَالْفَيْضِ الرَّحْمَانِي

Wa-l fayḍi-r-Rahmāni

And the out-pourings (of Mercy) from the all-Merciful

الَّذِي أَكْرَمْتَهُ بِالمِنَنِ الْقُرْآنِي

Alladhī akramtahu bi-l-minani-l-Qur'ānī

He is the one on whom you bestowed the bounties of Quran

وَالسَّبْعِ الْمَثَانِي

Wa-s-sab'i-l-mathāni

And the seven pairs

صَاحِبُ الْوَجُودِ النُّورَانِي

Ṣāḥibu-l-wajūdi-n-nūrānī
The one whose being is of light

والضَّوْءِ الرُّوْحَانِي

Wa-ḍ-ḍaw'i-r-rūḥānī
And the radiance of the spirit

وَالَّذِي أَيَّدْتَهُ بِالنَّصْرِ السُلْطَانِي

Wa-l-ladhī ayyadtahu bi-n-naṣri-s-sulṭānī
And the one whom you supported with the sovereign assistance

وَالْمَقَامِ الْفَرْدَانِي

Wa-lmaqāmi-l-fardānī
And the stations of singleness

وَشَرَّفْتَهُ بِالْخَتْمِ الْبُرْهَانِي

Wa sharraftahu bi-l-khatmi-l-burhānī
And you ennobled him with seal of authenticity

وَالْفَتْحِ الرَّبَّانِي

Wa-l-fatḥi-r-Rabbānī
And the opening of Lordship

طَلْسَمُ الرَّحْمَةِ

Ṭalsamu-r-Raḥmah

The formula of Mercy

وَسَلِّمْ تَسْلِيمًا

Wa sallim taslīmā

O Allah shower him with blessings of peace.

يَا بَاقِي يَا حَيُّ

Yā Bāqī Yā Ḥayy **50**
O Everlasting, O Ever Living

يَا مَنْ تَعَاظَمَ

YA MAN TA'AZAMA

O YOU MOST MAGNIFICIENT

by Ahmad bin 'Ali Al-Rifa'i Al-Kabir

This poem in praise of God's magnificence was composed by the 6th century Sufi master, Ahmad bin 'Ali Al-Rifa'i Al-Kabir. He was born in the month of Muḥarram 500 Ḥijri and passed away in the first half of Rajab, year 578, at Umm Ubaidah in Iraq, where he was also born. Many historians have depicted him as very humble, clean hearted individual, who was also a jurist of the *Shāfi'ī* school.

The grandson of Ibn Al-Jawzi said: "I spent the night of the half of *Sha'bān*, and there were about 100,000 people with him. I said to him, "What a large gathering!" He replied: "May God raise me with Hamam if I ever see myself as the leader of these people!"

The beauty of this poem lies in the manner in which the author captured the connection between perplexity in face of God's magnificence, and the love which arises out of that perplexity (*ḥayrā'*). In it, the author relates his own experience of that perplexing love.

يَا مَنْ تَعَاظَمَ

O YOU MOST MAGNIFICIENT

RECITE EACH COUPLET TWICE

يَا مَنْ تَعَاظَمَ حَتَّى رَقَّ مَعْنَاهُ
وَلَا تَرَدَّى رِدَاءَ الْكِبْرِ إِلاَّ هُو

Ya man ta'āẓama ḥatta raqqa ma'nāhu
Wa lā taraddā ridā'a-l-kibri illā hu

O you who are so magnificent that your essence is infinitely subtle

تَاهُو بِحُبِّكَ أَقْوَامٌ وَأَنْتَ لَهُمْ
نِعْمَ الْحَبِيبُ وَإِنْ هَامُوا وَإِنْ تَاهُوا

Tāhū biḥubbika aqwāmun wa anta lahum
Ni'ma-l-habību wa inhāmū wa intāhū

People have become lost in your love,
Nonetheless you are always for them the best beloved
notwithstanding their rapture and their loss.

وَلِي حَبِيبٌ عَزِيزٌ لَا أَبُوحُ بِهِ
أَخْشَى فَضِيحَةَ وَجْهِي يَوْمَ أَلْقَاهُ

Wa lī ḥabībun 'azīzun la abūḥu bihi
Akhshā faḍiḥata wajhi yawma alqāhu

I have a precious lover but I will not disclose about Him,
I fear lest my face be cast down on the day I meet Him

أُغَالِطُ النَّاسَ طُرًّا فِي مَحَبَّتِهِ
وَلَيْسَ يَعْلَمُ مَا فِي الْقَلْبِ إِلَا هُو

Ughāliṭu-n-nāsa ṭurran fī maḥabbatihi
Wa laysa ya'alamu mā fi-l-qalbi illā hu

I make believe to every one regarding His love,
No one knows what hearts conceal except Him.

قَالُوا أَتَنْسَى الَّذِي تَهْوَى فَقُلْتُ لَهُمْ
يَا قَوْمِي مَنْ هُوَ رُوحِي كَيْفَ أَنْسَاه

Qālū atansā-ladhī tahwā faqultu lahum
Ya Qawmī man huwa rūhī kayfa ansāhu

They said, do you forget the one you love: I said to them:
O my people, how could I forget the one who is my spirit.

وَكَيْفَ أَنْسَاهُ وَالْأَشْيَاءُ بِهِ حَسُنَتْ
مِنَ الْعَجَائِبِ يَنْسَى الْعَبْدُ مَوْلَاهُ

Wa kayfa ansāhu wa-l-ashyā'u bihi ḥasunat
Mina-l-'ajā'ibi yansa-l-'abdu mawlāhu

How could I forget Him when by Him everything is made right
What a surprise that a servant could forget his Master

مَا غَابَ عَنِّي وَلَكِنْ لَسْتُ أَبْصُرُهُ
إِلَّا وَقُلْتُ جِهَارًا قَدْ هُوَ اللهُ

Ma ghāba 'annī wa lākin lastu abṣuruhu
Illā wa qultu jihāran qad huwa-Allāhu

I have never lost Him out of sight though whenever I see Him I say out loud, He indeed is Allah

مَاذَا يَقُولُ اللَّوَاحِي ضَلَّ سَعْيُهُمْ
وَمَاذَا تَقُولُ الْأَعَادِي زَادَ مَعْنَاهُ

Mādhā yaqūlu-l-lawāḥī ḍalla sa'yuhum
Wa mādhā taqūlu-l-a'ādī zāda ma'nāhu

What the chiders say for their efforts go in vain,
And what the enemies say only increase His sublimity

هَلْ غَيْرَ أَنِّي أَهْوَاهُ وَقَدْ صَدَقُوا
نَعْمُ نَعْمُ أَنَا أَهْوَاهُ وَأَهْوَاهُ

Hal ghayra 'annī ahwāhu wa qad ṣadaqū
Na'm na'm anā ahwāhu wa ahwāhu

All but because I love Him, yes they are right,
Yes, yes! I love Him and I love Him

أَسْتَغْفِرُ اللهَ إِلاَّ مِنْ مَحَبَّتِهِ
فَإِنَّهَا حَسَنَاتِي يَومَ أَلْقَاهُ

Astaghfiru-llāha min maḥabbatihi
Fa innahā hasanāti yawma alqāhu

I seek from Allah to redeem me from everything else except Love of Him,
For indeed that is what counts as my good deeds the day I meet Him

فَإِنْ يَقُولُوا بِأَنَّ الْحُبَّ مَعْصِيَةٌ
فَالْحُبُّ أَحْسَنُ مَا يُلْقَى بِهِ اللهُ

Fa'inna yaqūlū bi anna-l-ḥubba ma'ṣiyatun
Fa-l-ḥubbu aḥsanu mā yulqā bihi-llāhu

If they claim that love is error
Indeed love is the best thing to meet Allah with.

CONCLUSION

Closing Statements

This collection of litanies and prayers (*adhkār*) is concise, but comprehensive. It includes both attributes of beauty and majesty, as well as the Divine essence (*dhāt*[1]) in a beautiful blend set against a backdrop of prayers (*ṣalawāt*) on the Prophet, peace be upon him. These prayers are meant to induce tranquility (*sakīnah*) on the reciters to enable them to bear the weight and the impact of God's excellence, which would be otherwise unbearable.

1. Refers to the litany "*lā ilāha illallāh*"

About the Author

Raised in the time-honoured spiritual traditions of the Sahilian region of Senegambian West Africa, Imam Fode Drame is a unique teacher. He blends tradition with modernity, past with present, old with new, and in the end provides the seeker with the perfect tool to overcome his challenge and attain his or her quest. With this in mind, in 2005 Drame founded Zawiyah Foundation, a non-profit charitable organization, in Vancouver, Canada. The purpose of this foundation is to spread Drame's teaching about "accurate responding" locally and globally.

52539793R00023

Made in the USA
San Bernardino, CA
23 August 2017